M000318300

THE
GREEN
BOOK

M. AL GATHAFI

THE GREEN BOOK

The Solution to the Problem of Democracy

The Solution to the Economic Problem

The Social Basis of the Third Universal Theory

ITHACA
P R E S S

The Green Book

Published by
Ithaca Press
8 Southern Court, South Street
Reading RG1 4QS, UK
E-mail: enquiries@garnetpublishing.co.uk
Website: www.garnetpublishing.co.uk

First edition 2005

Hardback ISBN 0 86372 306 3
Paperback ISBN 0 86372 302 0

British Library Cataloguing-in-Publication Data. A catalogue record for
this book is available from the British Library.

Credits
Editor
Emma Hawker

Design
David Rose

Production
Typesetting: Samantha Barden

www.algathafi.org

greenbookstudies@hotmail.com

Part One

The Solution
to the Problem of Democracy

The Authority of the People: The Political Basis of the Third Universal Theory

The instrument of government

The instrument of government is the primary political problem facing human communities. This problem is often the reason behind family feuds and it was further aggravated to an alarming extent after the rise of modern societies.

People today are still faced by the persistent problem of the instrument of government. Failing to find the final and democratic solution to this political problem, many societies are bearing the burden of its far-reaching consequences and ramifications. *The Green Book* presents the ultimate solution to this problem.

All existing political systems in the world today are the product of the struggle for power between potential instruments of government. This struggle, whether conducted by peaceful or armed means, may be a class struggle, a sectarian or tribal strife, or a power struggle between individual adversaries vying for political ascendancy. It invariably culminates in the victory of one instrument of government – whether it be an individual, a sect, a political party or a social class – and the defeat of the people, the defeat of true democracy.

Political struggle which culminates in the victory of a candidate obtaining 51 per cent of the total votes of the electorate, establishes a dictatorship in the seat of power garbed in the guise of democracy. It is in fact, a dictatorship because 49 per cent of the electorate would then be governed by an instrument of government they did not vote for, and which has been imposed upon them. This is the essence of dictatorship. Moreover, a political conflict may culminate in the rise to power of an instrument of government representing a minority of the electorate. Such an outcome is the product of an electoral process whereby the votes of the electorate are distributed among a number of candidates, of whom one would obviously obtain a number of votes larger than the number obtained separately by any one of the other candidates. Yet, though the sum total of the votes scored by these other candidates would be the largest and represent a sweeping majority, the candidate who independently scored the highest percentage of the ballot, which is comparatively the lowest, is legally considered a winner in a democratically conducted elections. In actual fact, such an outcome heralds the rise of a dictatorship in the misleading guise of democracy.

Such is the reality of political systems of government prevalent in our world today: sheer dictatorship falsifying true democracy.

Parliaments

No representation of the people – representation is a falsehood.

The institution of parliament in the world today is the backbone of modern traditional democracy. Yet such an institution is a misrepresentation of the people, and parliamentary systems are a contrived solution to the problem of democracy.

Parliaments as instruments of government are essentially established in the name of the people. Yet this underlying principle is in itself undemocratic, since democracy as a system of government means the power of the people, and not power vested in elected members of an assembly, in the name of the people. As such, the mere existence of parliaments underlies the absence of the people, for democracy can only exist with the presence of the people and not in the presence of representatives of the people.

> Parliament is a governing body in absentia.

Parliaments have become a legal barrier between people and their right to exercise authority. They exclude the masses in order to prevent them from practising politics, and monopolize the control of politics in their name. The people are left with nothing but a semblance of democracy, manifested in the long queues of voters waiting their turn to cast their votes in the ballot box.

To unravel the real nature of parliaments, we must know how they are formed. They are either elected from constituencies, a political party or a coalition of parties, or are appointed. All such methods are undemocratic. The division of the population into constituencies means that a member of parliament represents thousands, hundreds of thousands, even millions of citizens, depending on the population count. It also means that a member of parliament thus elected keeps few people's organizational links with the electorate, and is considered, along with the other members, a representative of the people as a whole. This method is a requirement of existing traditional democracies. At this point in the process, the masses and the elected member of parliament, are totally set apart, and the elected member, upon obtaining the majority vote, becomes a monopolizer of the people's sovereignty by virtue of the authority vested in him to manage their affairs.

Traditional democracy, prevalent in our world today, confers upon members of parliament a sanctity and an immunity it denies ordinary citizens. Parliaments have thus become a means of confiscating and monopolizing the power of the people. Such a state of affairs gives the people the right to struggle, by waging a revolution to destroy these instruments – the so-called representative assemblies which monopolize democracy and sovereignty, and usurp the will of the masses. The masses will rise and proclaim the new principle in a thundering cry: "No, to representation of the people."

Representative assemblies are a misrepresentation of democracy.

If a parliament is formed from members who are followers of one particular political party as a result of their electoral victory, then this parliament is not representative of the people, but of this particular party; the executive body it will appoint will be the executive power of this party, and not of the people.

Similarly, a parliament of proportional representation whose seats are distributed to the different parties according to their percentage success in the vote is not representative of the people: its members do not represent the people but their parties; and the ruling power established by this coalition of the parties is the power of the coalition and not of the people.

Under such systems, the people are the prey fought over by the predators: instruments of government compete in their power struggle for the votes of the people they in turn neglect and exploit, while the people move silently towards the ballot box, like the beads in a rosary, to cast their votes in the same way that they throw rubbish in dustbins. This is traditional democracy that is prevalent in the world today, regardless of the system of government in place and regardless of whether it is a one-party, a bipartisan or a multi-party system, or indeed a regime which precludes political parties. Traditional democracy therefore represents forms of government in which the principle of representation is a fraud.

Assemblies whose seats are allotted to heirs and other privileged appointees cannot be similarly categorized: they lack even a semblance of democracy.

Moreover, the electoral system in the so-called democratic forms of government is a demagogic practice in the literal sense of the word. It is based on propaganda campaigns aimed at winning over the constituents, and involves buying and manipulating votes. This produces closed election campaigns which the poor cannot afford to participate in and thus the rich are always elected.

The principle of elected representation was advocated by philosophers, intellectuals and writers in times past, when people were unwittingly herded like sheep by sultans, emperors and conquerors. At that time, what the people truly aspired to was to have someone to represent them to the rulers. Even when this aspiration was rejected, throughout history people have waged a bitter and protracted struggle to attain this goal. After the triumph of republicanism and the beginning of the era of the masses, it is unthinkable that the concept of democracy should be translated into an electoral process whereby a few elected deputies are mandated to represent the masses. This is an outdated theory, and an obsolete experiment. Power should be entirely for all the people. It should always be borne in mind that the most tyrannical of dictatorships the world has known have existed under the aegis of parliaments.

The political party

The political party is a contemporary form of dictatorship. It is the latest modern dictatorial instrument of government, whereby the part rules the whole. Comprised of a group as opposed to an individual, a political party is able nevertheless to attribute a semblance of democracy to itself through the formation of councils and committees, and through the propaganda activities of its members.

But a political party is not in any respect a democratic instrument. It is an organization formed by individuals who share the same interests, ideas, culture, place or doctrine. They come together to form a political party so that they may realize their interests or impose their ideas or the might of their doctrine on society as a whole, with the intention of seizing power as a means to implement their political program.

Democratically, none of these individuals or members of a political party should rule over a whole people who constitute diverse interests, opinions, dispositions, places and beliefs. A political party is a dictatorial instrument of government which enables those with the same ideas or interests to rule over the people as a whole. In actual fact the party constitutes only a small minority.

The purpose of organizing a political party is to create an instrument with which to govern the people, the non-party members of the populace.

Fundamentally, political parties are based on a domineering and despotic theory: the manipulation of the people by the party leadership. The leadership alleges that its rise to power is a means to realizing the party's objectives, and assumes that its objectives also represent the aspirations of the people.

Such theorizing is a justification for party dictatorship, and it is the theory presented by any dictatorship.

Regardless of their diversity, political parties set forth theories that are basically the same. Yet it is the plurality of parties that escalates the struggle for power which usually supersedes and destroys any achievements gained by the people, and also subverts any socially beneficial plans. Such destruction and subversion is meant to justify the opposition party's attempts to undermine the ruling party it aims to replace.

In their fight against each other, political parties seldom engage in armed strife; instead they usually resort to mud-slinging tactics to discredit one another. Their battle inevitably rages beyond society's vital and prime interests, and of these some, if not all, may fall victim of this wrangling and be destroyed. However, this situation serves to support the arguments of the opposition parties against the ruling party or coalition.

In order to rule, the opposition party must defeat the existing instrument of government. To do so, the opposition must undermine the government's achievements and cast doubts on its plans, even if these plans were beneficial to society, to prove the incompetence of the current governing instrument. Consequently, the interests and programs of society become the victims of the power struggle raging among the political parties.

Although the struggle for power among political parties stimulates political activity, it nevertheless has a devastating impact on political, social and economic levels. Invariably, it culminates in the triumph of just another instrument of power – in the downfall of one political party and the rise of another – but also in the defeat of the people, and thus the defeat of democracy. It should be added here that political parties can also be bribed or corrupted by both internal and external interests.

Initially, a political party is formed to represent the people. However it does not take long for the party leadership to become the representative of the party members, then for the head of the party to become the representative of the elite. It is clear that this is a game of deceitful farce based on a false form of democracy, which has underlying selfish and authoritarian intentions that are fraudulently pursued with manoeuvring and political games. This confirms the fact that the party system is a modern instrument of dictatorship which the world has not yet eradicated. It is the dictatorship of the modern age.

> A political party represents a portion of the people, but the sovereignty of the people is indivisible.

When a parliament is formed by a winning political party, it becomes an assembly representative of this party, and the executive power formed by such an assembly becomes the party's instrument of authority over the people. Thus, the party which is supposed to exercise power in the interest of all the people, is actually the arch-enemy of a large proportion of the people, namely the party or parties of the opposition and their supporters. This does not make the opposition the popular guardian watching over the performance of the ruling party, but rather it is itself lying in wait for the opportunity to replace it. The legal guardian watching over the ruling party, according to the principles of modern democracy, is parliament. But since members of the ruling party constitute the majority in parliament, supervision of the ruling party's performance in government comes from within its own party, i.e. the ruling party supervises itself. This state of affairs illustrates the deceit, falseness and invalidity of the political theories prevalent in the world today, and it is these which are the source of contemporary traditional democracy.

The political party is the modern-day equivalent of the tribe or sect. A society which is ruled by a one-party system is similar to a society which is governed by one tribe or one sect, because, as noted above, a political party represents the vision of one group, or the interests of one social group, or one belief or place, and therefore represents a minority of the people. Similarly, a tribe or a sect represents a minority of the people, and has its own particular interests or belief from which its vision is formed. While the blood tie constitutes the only difference between a tribe and a political party, indeed a tribe could have been the basis for the foundation of a party. There is no difference between a political party's struggle for power and a tribal or sectarian struggle for power. Just as a tribal or sectarian regime is politically condemned and rejected, a political party regime should likewise be condemned and rejected: they all follow the same course which leads to the same outcome. The impact of the struggle of political parties on society is as damaging and devastating as that of any tribal or sectarian struggle.

> A political party rules in the name of the people, but in truth there is no representation in lieu of the people.

The social class

The class political system is the same as a party, a tribal or a sectarian political system. It is a political system whereby a particular social class dominates a society in the same way as a political party, tribe or sect would.

Social classes, like political parties, sects or tribes, are groups of people bound together by common interests. Common interests emerge from the existence of a particular group of people bound together by kinship, place, belief, culture, or standard of living. Classes, parties, sects and tribes emerge because kinship, belief, standard of living, culture or place create a common view point as to how their common interests are best achieved. Thus social structures whether classes, parties, tribes or sects emerge and eventually a political instrument develops from these which is used to realize the common vision and interests of that particular group. However, the people are neither a class, party, tribe nor sect, for these represent only a section of the people and constitute a minority in society. If either a class, party, tribe or sect dominates a society then the system of government becomes a dictatorship. Nevertheless, a class or a tribal coalition is preferable to a coalition of parties, since societies are almost invariably descendants of tribes. It is rare to come across a people without tribal roots, and whilst all people belong to different social classes, they are not all affiliated to political parties; but political parties or coalitions represent a minority compared to the masses outside their membership. Moreover, in a true democracy, there is no justification for one social class to suppress other classes in order to serve its own interests. Likewise there is no justification for one political party to suppress other parties for its own benefit, nor for one tribe or sect to do the same.

Condoning such actions means spurning the principles of democracy and justifies the use of force. Such policies of suppression are dictatorial as they are against the interest of society as a whole. It is an unjustifiable course of action because society is not made up of one social class, one tribe or one sect, or of members of one political party; it is made up of several interest groups, of which one group is intent on eliminating all other groups in its attempt to prevail.

Such actions do not serve the interests of society as a whole but the interest of one social class, tribe, sect or political party, who is intent on ruling the society. Basically this is an act of elimination directed against all members of society who do not belong to the party, the social class, tribe or sect which is carrying out the policy of elimination. A society torn apart by party wrangling is no different from a society torn apart by tribal or sectarian conflicts.

A political party established to represent a social class inevitably becomes a substitute of this class. This gradual process of transformation continues until the political party finally becomes the successor to the social class, and is hostile to the class whose interests it supposedly represents.

Any social class which inherits a society also inherits its characteristics. Thus, if the working class were to subdue all other social classes in a society, it inherits the society and it forms its material and social base. The heir acquires the traits of those from whom it inherits although this may not be apparent immediately. Over time, however, the characteristics of the other crushed social classes will manifest themselves within the ranks of the working class itself. Those members who have acquired these characteristics will accordingly assume the attitudes appropriate to their newly evolved characteristics. Eventually the working class becomes a society in its own right, burdened with the same contradictions which existed in the former society. At first, the spiritual and material standards of individuals become unequal. Then factions will emerge and then automatically become different social classes – the same social classes which were previously eliminated. Finally, the struggle for power in the society begins again. Initially, it was a struggle among groups of individuals, but with time, this develops into a struggle among factions, which then escalates into a new class struggle in which each social class attempts to become the instrument of power.

Being social in nature, the material basis of any society is changeable. The instrument of government may be stable for a certain period of time, but eventually it breaks down as new material and social standards evolve and emerge from the same material basis. Class struggles have erupted in the past in societies made up of only one social class. But inevitably evolution leads to the emergence of other social classes in society. The social class which takes over and possesses another class in order to secure its own instrument of government in the seat of power, will eventually discover that it is as vulnerable to the influences of property and possession as society itself is.

In conclusion, all attempts at unifying the material basis of a society in order to solve the problem of government or to put an end to the struggle in favour of one particular political party, social class, sect, or tribe have failed. In addition, all attempts to appease the masses by having them elect their representatives, or by seeking their opinions in referendums, have also failed. To persist in such attempts is a waste of time and makes a mockery of the people.

Referendums

Referendums make a mockery of democracy.

Referendums make a mockery of democracy. The people who respond with "yes" or "no" are not actually expressing their will, but rather are constrained to respond as such because the concept of modern democracy so dictates. They are only allowed to select one of two words: either "yes" or "no". Referendums represent the most extreme repressive dictatorships. Individuals who respond with a "no" should be able to state their reasons for this response and why they refrained from responding with a "yes". Similarly, individuals who respond with a "yes" should be given the opportunity to justify their agreement and explain why they did not choose to give "no" as an answer. Each should be able to speak out and give the reasons for agreement or disagreement.

> *Individuals must have the opportunity to justify their opinions.*

Which path then should human communities follow in order to be permanently rid of tyranny and dictatorship?

The intricate problem with democracy is reflected in the problems with the instruments of government, which in turn are demonstrated by the conflicts of partisans, individuals and classes. Referendums and election processes were actually devised to cover up the failure of these unsuccessful experiments to solve this problem. Nevertheless, a solution is attainable. It lies in finding an instrument of government other than those subject to the struggle for power, and which represents only one faction in society, that is to say an instrument of government which is neither a political party, a social class, a sect nor a tribe, but is an instrument of government which encompasses the people as a whole. In other words we are looking for an instrument of government which neither represents the people or acts on their behalf. There can be no representation of the people and representation is a fraud. If this instrument of government were found, the problem would be solved and true people's democracy would be established. In this way humankind would bring to an end the eras of tyranny and dictatorship, replacing them with the will of the people.

The Green Book presents the ultimate solution to the problem of the instrument of governance and indicates the course that the masses should follow if they are to leave behind the eras of dictatorship to enter the era of genuine democracy. This new theory is based on the authority of the people and it renounces representation or delegation of authority. It leads to the achievement of direct, orderly and efficient democracy, unlike previous attempts at direct democracy which proved to be inapplicable, as they had disregarded the need for people's organization at the lower levels of society.

People's Conferences and People's Committees

> There is no democracy without people's conferences.

People's Conferences are the only means to achieve people's democracy. Any form of government contrary to this method is undemocratic. In our world today, all existing forms of government are undemocratic; they still stray away from the course which leads to the establishment of People's Conferences: the culmination of the journey of the masses to achieve democracy.

People's Conferences and People's Committees are the ultimate accomplishment of the people's struggle for democracy. They are not products of the imagination; they are the product of thought which has assimilated all experiences of humanity in its pursuit of democracy.

In fact, direct democracy is the ideal and indisputable method of government. But the virtual impossibility of gathering all the people together at once in order to discuss, consider and decide their politics, has caused nations to depart from this concept of direct democracy, which has therefore remained an utopian ideal far removed from reality. Various other theories of government have been applied as substitutes (parliamentary assemblies, party coalitions and referendums) but they all led to the isolation of the masses, who were excluded from running their own affairs and robbed of their sovereignty. The endless succession of governing instruments – the individual, the social class, the sect, the tribe or political parties constantly in a state of power struggle – have monopolized the rights of the masses and stripped them of their sovereignty.

The Green Book shows the masses the way to direct democracy based on a magnificent and practical system: the Third Universal Theory. This theory is based on actual experience with direct democracy, an ideal over which no two reasonable adults can possibly disagree, although the method of implementation of which was previously inconceivable.

The Third Universal Theory permanently solves the problem of democracy in our world and it is up to the masses to struggle to eliminate the various forms of existing dictatorships,

Committees everywhere.

be they parliament, sect, tribe or class, in one-party, two-party or multi-party systems of government, which all inappropriately call themselves democracies.

There is only one theory and one method of true democracy. The dissimilarity and diversity of the forms of government claiming to be democratic is evidence enough that they are not. The authority of the people has just one face, and this can only be realized by one method – the establishment of People's Conferences and People's Committees everywhere. Without these, democracy is unattainable.

Firstly, the people are divided into Basic People's Conferences. Each of these selects it own secretariat. The secretariats of all the People's Conferences together form Conferences other than the Basic People's Conferences.

The masses of the Basic People's Conferences will then select administrative People's Committees to replace government administration. From then on, all public institutions will be run by People's Committees which will be answerable to Basic People's Conferences which dictate policies and oversee their implementation. Thus, both the administration and supervision become the people's responsibility and the outdated definition of democracy – democracy is the supervision of the government by the people – is finally done away with. It is replaced by the true definition: democracy is the supervision of the people by the people.

All citizens who are members of these People's Conferences belong by virtue of employment or profession to different social groups, and therefore must set up their own Professional People's Conferences in addition to being, by virtue of citizenship, members of the Basic People's Conferences or People's Committees. All issues dealt with by the People's Conferences and People's Committees are drafted in their final version in the General People's Conference, which is attended by the secretariats of the People's Conferences and People's Committees. Resolutions of the General People's Conference are submitted for implementation to the People's Conferences and People's Committees, which are in turn answerable to the Basic People's Conferences.

It should be noted that the General People's Conference is not like a parliament, a mere congregation of members or persons, but rather it is the gathering together of the People's Conferences and People's Committees.

In this way the problem of the instrument of government is solved, and the dictatorial instruments of power finally disappear. The people become the sole instrument of government and the dilemma of democracy in our world is finally resolved.

The authority of the people

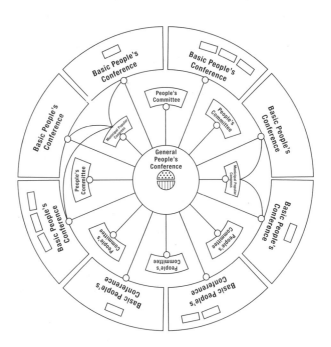

Key

General Secretariat of the
General People's Conference

General People's Committee

Secretariat of the Conference

People's Committee for the
Various Executive Sectors
(agriculture, housing, health
etc.)

Professional People's
Conferences

The legislation of society

The legislation of society is another problem closely connected to the problem of the instruments of government which has not yet been resolved. Although solutions were found for this problem at certain periods of history the problem still exists today.

It is invalid and undemocratic for a committee or an assembly to be empowered to pass legislation for society, or for an individual, a committee or an assembly to amend or abrogate legislation.

What then is the legislation of society? Who passes this legislation? What is its relevance to democracy?

Natural legislation in any society is grounded in either religion or customs, and any attempt to make legislation for a given society derived from sources other than these two is invalid and illogical. Constitutions cannot be considered as the legislation of society. A constitution is a man-made law, which needs to be ascribed to particular sources for its vindication – it does not have a natural source. The problem of freedom in modern times is that constitutions have become the legislation of society, and are based solely on the views of the dictatorial instruments of government existing in the world today – autocracies, party dictatorships and others. This is evident in the diversity of the various constitutions which exist: yet man's freedom is one and the same throughout the world. The reason for this diversity is the variation in views held by the diverse instruments of government. This is how freedom becomes vulnerable under the contemporary political systems that exist in the world. The methods chosen by instruments of government to control their people are incorporated into constitutions which people are constrained to obey by the force of

> Man's freedom is one and the same throughout the world.

laws derived from the same constitutions which are in turn, are derived from the views and dispositions of the instruments of government.

The norms of the dictatorial instruments of government have replaced the norms of nature: man-made law has replaced natural law and, as a result, criteria have been lost. Man is essentially one and the same everywhere physically and in terms of sensibility, and that is the reason why natural law is the logical law for mankind. Constitutions as man-made laws do not consider man as one. This view has no justification, except for the fact that it represents the will of the instrument of government (an individual, a parliament, a social class or a political party) to control and manipulate the people. The fact that constitutions change with the instruments of government corroborates this in that they reflect the disposition of the instruments of government, and are drafted for their benefit, and are not inspired by natural law.

> Natural law is the logical law for man

The imminent danger threatening freedom lies in the absence of the real legislation of society which has been substituted with man-made laws. These legislations are instituted in order to vindicate the ruling method adopted by the instruments of government, instead of being adapted to suit the fundamental legislation of society. The importance of this legislation, which is not man-made, is in its being the criterion used to distinguish between right and wrong, between what is true and what is false, and between the rights of individuals and their responsibilities. Freedom becomes threatened when society lacks a sacred legislation of confirmed statutes, not liable to change or substitution by any instrument of government. It is rather the responsibility of the instruments of government to conform to the legislation of society. Unfortunately throughout the world people today are governed by man-made legislations which are liable to be changed or abrogated depending on the power struggle among the competing instruments of government.

Holding a referendum for the people to vote on the constitution is not sufficient. Referendums are in themselves a falsification of democracy; they allow a response of only one word, either a "yes" or a "no". People are compelled by man-made law to vote thus in a referendum. However a referendum on the constitution does not necessarily make the constitution the legislation of society – it remains just a constitution, the subject of a referendum, and nothing more.

The legislation of society is an everlasting human legacy, and as such, it is not the property of the living alone. Hence, to draft a constitution and request the people's vote of approval, is a mockery.

Codes of man-made laws derived from man-made constitutions are abundant with physical punitive measures against man, whereas customs contain few such measures. Customs call for spiritual non-physical but deserving punitive measures. These customs are inherent in religion, in which most physical punishments are postponed punishments, and most judgements are passed as exhortations, guiding instructions and answers to questions, making them the most appropriate legislation which is respectful of human beings. In religion, immediate punitive measures are taken only in extreme cases for the benefit of society.

Religion embraces customs and customs are an expression of the natural life of the people. Therefore, religion is an affirmation of natural legislation. Non-religious legislation and legislation which is not derived from customs, are inventions of man against man. These are therefore invalid since they are not derived from the natural sources of customs and religion.

Who oversees the progress of society?

The question arises: who oversees the progress of society and warns of any deviations from the legislation of society when they occur?

In a democracy, no one group can claim the right to do this on behalf of society as society is its own overseer. Any such claim by an individual or a group is dictatorial because democratically this is the responsibility of the society as a whole. Democracy means all society overseeing its own progress. This can be achieved through the democratic instrument of government which results from the self-organization of society into Basic People's Conferences, and from the government of these people through People's Conferences and People's Committees then the General People's Conference (the National Conference), the occasion when secretariats of the People's Conferences and the People's Committees convene. According to this theory, the people are the instrument of government, and as such, they are their own overseer. In this manner society thus becomes by itself, the overseer of its legislation.

How does society rectify its course in case of any deviation from its legislation?

When the instrument of government is a dictatorship, which is the case of existing political systems in the world today, a society, aware of deviations from the legislation, has no means to express its position and rectify the situation other than through violence. It has no other option but to rise in revolt against the instrument of government in the seat of power. However, even if violence or revolution are expressions of society's attitude towards such deviations, participation in the uprising would not involve the whole of society. It would be an act undertaken only by those who are capable of such an initiative and possess the courage to be outspoken and pronounce the will of society. Yet, a popular uprising would in itself constitute a dictatorial incident because this revolutionary initiative shall necessarily create opportune circumstances for another instrument of government to rise to power in the name of the people. In other words, the instrument of power would still be a dictatorship.

Violence and the use of force as instruments of change are undemocratic, but they happen as an outcome of the development of an undemocratic condition. Any society which still finds itself in this vicious circle is a backward society. How is this then to be resolved?

The solution is for the people to become the instrument of government – to organize themselves into Basic People's Conferences and People's Committees to replace the governmental administration, and convene the General People's Conference as a periodic national gathering for the Conferences and Committees. In such a system, any deviation from the legislation of society would be dealt with through the democratic process rather than through the use of force. This process is not a voluntary choice of the method to amend or change the state of affairs in society, but is an inevitable result of the nature of the democratic system in which no outside group exists who can thus be rendered a target of violent action or held responsible for any deviations.

The media

Democracy is popular rule not popular expression.

Freedom of expression is the right of every natural person, even if a person chooses to behave irrationally to express his or her insanity. It is also the right of corporate bodies to freely express their corporate identity as such. However, individuals in both cases express only themselves. A private individual represents only himself and a corporate body represents only the status of the group of individuals that make up that corporate body. Therefore, when an individual expresses himself as insane for example, it does not mean that the rest of society is insane. An individual's expression is his own alone, and a corporate body's expression expresses only the interests or viewpoint of the group. A tobacco producing or distributing company for example expresses the interests of the parties comprising the company, i.e. those who are making profit from producing or selling tobacco, although it is hazardous to health.

The press is society's medium of expression, not an individual's or corporate body's medium of expression. Therefore, it cannot be logically or democratically the private property of such persons. Any newspaper privately owned by an individual is a medium expressing only the views of this individual. To claim that it expresses public opinion is false and groundless because it expresses the views of one individual. However, while it is democratically not permissible for an individual to own any information or publishing medium, all individuals have a natural right to self-expression by any means, even if such means were insane and meant to prove a person's insanity. On the other hand, a newspaper published by members of a certain profession, is a medium of expression exclusive to this professional group. It presents their own points of view and not that of the general public. This applies to all other corporate and private individuals in society.

The democratic press is the mass media published and broadcast by a People's Committee, comprising members from all the various groups in society without exception. Only in this case, and in no other situation, will the press or any other information medium be democratic, expressing the viewpoints of society as a whole, representing all its various groups. If members of the medical profession publish a journal, then this journal must necessarily be a purely medical publication. This same condition applies to all other professions. While individuals have a natural right to self-expression, the principles of democracy do not give individuals the right to express anyone else's opinions. Only in this manner is the so-called problem of the freedom of the press radically and democratically solved.

The problem of the freedom of the press, which is still a controversial problem the world over, persists as a result of the problem of democracy in general, and no solution can be found unless the crisis of democracy is entirely resolved in any given society. The only way to resolve the intricate problem of democracy is by applying the Third Universal Theory.

According to this theory, the democratic system is a cohesive structure whose foundation stones are firmly laid one above the other, the Basic People's Conferences, the People's Conferences, and the People's Committees, which finally come together when the General People's Conference convenes. There is absolutely no conception of a democratic society other than this.

To summarize, the era of the masses, rapidly advancing towards us to overtake the era of republics, excites the emotions and dazzles the eyes. But in as much as it heralds the advent of real freedom for the masses and the blissful emancipation from the chains of all instruments of government, it is also the harbinger of a chaotic and tumultuous era if the new democracy – the authority of the people – were to suffer a relapse. Such an era would bring back autocracy, or the rule of one social class, tribe, sect or political party.

> *Those who are strongest in society govern.*

Theoretically, this is genuine democracy, but in reality, the strong always rule: that is to say those who are strongest in society hold the reigns of government.

Part Two

The Solution
to the Economic Problem

Socialism:
The Economic Basis of the
Third Universal Theory

Important historical developments took place in the course of attempts to solve the problem of work and wages, the relationship between employers and employees, owners and producers. These developments led to concessions which determined fixed working hours, overtime pay, leaves of absence, minimum wages, profit-sharing, workers' participation in management, the prohibition of arbitrary dismissals, social security, the right to strike, and other provisions contained in almost all contemporary labour laws. Of no less significance are developments with respect to the issue of property, with the establishment of systems of government which set limits to income, and prohibited private property, transferring ownership to the state.

Despite all these important developments in the history of economics, the deep-rooted economic problem still fundamentally exists despite all the refinements, improvements and developments, even though it has been made less severe than in past centuries and has given workers many benefits. Attempts to address the issue of property have failed to resolve the problems of producers. They are still wage earners, although the right of private property, incontestable in regimes of the extreme right, was amended and changed in centrist regimes and regimes of the extreme left.

Attempts to improve wages did not fare any better, although the end result of such attempts granted workers concessions which are guaranteed by legislation and safeguarded by trade unions. With the advent of the Industrial Revolution the miserable conditions of the producers changed and workers, technicians and administrators acquired rights which at one time seemed unattainable. In reality, however, the economic problem still exists.

Attempts made to settle the issue of wages failed to resolve the problem; they were deceitful and reformist attempts that were more like donations to charity rather than recognition of the rights of workers. Why are workers rewarded with wages? Because they produce a product for the benefit of others who hire them to produce that product. In this case, workers do not consume what they produce but surrender it in return for a wage. Hence the sound rule is that *"he who produces consumes."*

Wage earners are but slaves to the masters who hire them. They are temporary slaves, and their servitude lasts as long as the duration of their work for which they receive wages from their employers (whether these are individuals or the state).

> Wage earners are a kind of slave, even if their wages improve.

The workers' relationship to the owner or the productive establishment and to their own interests is similar in all cases throughout the world, despite the differences between the laws governing property. Even state-owned economic enterprises give workers wages and other social benefits which are more like charitable offerings donated by rich owners of private economic establishments to their employees.

To claim that income from a state-controlled establishment is re-injected into society, and thus benefits the workers, as opposed to income from a privately-owned establishment which benefits solely the owner, is a true statement only if the general welfare of the society and private well-being of the workers is taken into account. Also we would have to assume that the political authority controlling ownership are the People's Conferences and People's Committees and not the authority of one social class, political party, coalition of parties, tribe, sect, family or individual, or any form of representative authority. As far as their own interests are concerned, the workers' immediate benefits in the form of wages, percentage of profits or social benefits, are the same as those received by workers in privately-owned corporations. That is to say, workers employed in state-controlled establishments and in private enterprises are all wage earners regardless of the status of the employer.

Thus, the developments which led to the transfer of property from private individuals to the state have not resolved the problem of the producer's right to benefit directly from what he produces, not indirectly through society, or in return for a wage. This failure is evident in the fact that producers are still wage earners in spite of the change in the legal status of property.

The ultimate solution to this problem is to abolish the wage system, emancipate the human being enslaved by it, and revert to the natural laws which defined relationships between workers and employers before the emergence of social classes and the development of various forms of government and man-made laws. These natural rules are the only measures that ought to govern human relations. These natural rules have produced a natural form of socialism based on equality among the components of economic production, and have maintained public consumption almost equal to natural production among individuals. The exploitation of man by man and the

> The ultimate solution is to abolish the wage system.

possession by some individuals of wealth exceeding personal needs, are manifestations of departure from the natural rule. This signals the beginning of corruption and distortion in the life of the human community, and is the beginning of the emergence of the exploitative society.

If we analyze the factors of economic production from ancient times up to the present, we shall find that they essentially consist of certain basic production components: the raw materials, the means of production and the producer. The natural rule of equality stipulates that each of these components is apportioned a share of this production, because the withdrawal of one negates production, and each is assigned an essential role in the process of production without which production is brought to a halt. Since each element is necessary and essential then all elements are equally important to the process of production, and should therefore have equal rights in the produced product. The pre-dominance of one over the other would be in conflict with the natural rule of equality and an infringement on the right of the other. Hence, for each element a share regardless of its nature. If a process of production is made with only two elements, then each should have half the produced product; if it is made with three elements, then each should have one-third of the produced product, and so on and so forth.

If we employ this natural rule in order to examine what actually happened in the past and what happens now we shall find the following. At the stage of manual production, the production process comprised the raw materials and a producer. Later, new means of production were introduced into the equation and used by man in the production process. Good examples of this are animals used as a unit of force. Gradually the machine replaced animals, and raw materials developed from simple and cheap materials to more complex and expensive materials. Likewise, man developed too: from an ordinary worker to skilled workers and engineers; their former large numbers dwindling to a few specialized technicians.

Even though the change in the components was both quantitative and qualitative, their essential role in the production process has remained basically unaltered. For example iron ore, as a component of production past and present, was manufactured primitively by blacksmiths into knives, axes and spears. Today, engineers manufacture iron ore in foundries, to produce various kinds of machinery, engines and motors. Beasts, like horses, oxen and camels, were replaced as elements of production by large factories and huge machines. Production, based upon primitive tools is now founded upon sophisticated technical instruments. Yet, the basic natural elements of production are essentially still the same despite the tremendous development, and this essential endurance confirms the natural rule as the proper and inevitable formula for the final solution of the economic problem, in view of the failure of all previous historical attempts which persistently ignored the application of natural rules.

All previous historical theories tackled the economic problem solely from the angle of ownership of one of the components of production, and solely from the angle of wages in return for production. This did not solve the real problem: the problem of production itself. Thus, the most prominent feature of the present economic systems in the world is a system of wages that deprives the workers of any right to the products they produce, regardless of whether this production is made for the benefit of society or the benefit of a private enterprise.

An industrial production plant comprises production material, machinery and workers, and production results from the utilization of the plant's machinery by the workers, to manufacture goods from raw materials. The manufactured goods, ready for use or consumption, are thus products of a production process that would not have taken place without the raw materials, the plant or the workers. If the raw materials were excluded, the factory would have nothing to produce; if the factory were excluded, nothing could be made of the raw materials; and if the workers were excluded, the factory would not operate. These three elements are equally essential for the production process and production is not possible without all three. Any one element of the three cannot possibly activate the production process on its own; neither can any two elements produce without the third. The natural rule in this case necessitates that each component receives an equal share of the benefits of production. In other words, the production of this factory is to be divided into three equal shares for each element of production, because what is important is not only the factory in itself but those who consume its product as well.

The same is applicable to agricultural production which involves only two components, man and the land, with the exclusion of the third component, the machine, and which is exactly like handicraft production. In this case production is divided into two shares only. If a piece of machinery is used in the process then production is divided, into three shares: the land, the agricultural worker and the machine. Thus, a socialist system is established whereby all processes of production are governed by such a natural rule.

The producers are the workers. They are called thus because the term "workers" or "labourers" is no longer realistic. Workers, as traditionally defined, are changing quantitatively and qualitatively, and the working class is constantly declining proportionately to the development of science and technology. Tasks that previously required a certain number of workers are now undertaken by a machine whose operation requires a lesser number of workers. This is the quantitative change of the labour force. As for the qualitative change, this is evident in the fact that the machine requires technical skill instead of muscular power. This is the change that the labour force has undergone.

The labour force has become a component of the production process. As a result of progress, the working force is no longer a multitude of illiterate labourers but has transformed into a limited number of technicians, engineers and scientists. Consequently, trade unions will disappear and be replaced by syndicates of engineers and technicians. Scientific progress is an irreversible gain for humanity. Thanks to this, illiteracy will be eliminated by this progress and the ordinary unskilled labour force will become a temporary phenomenon, bounded to disappear gradually. However, even in this new environment human beings will always remain the basic component in the production process.

Need

The freedom of a human being is always compromised if his or her needs are controlled by another, for need may lead to the enslavement of one person by another. Furthermore it is the cause of exploitation. Need is a real problem, and conflict is provoked as a result of one man's needs being controlled by another.

In need no freedom indeed.

Housing

> Masters in their
> own homes.

Private dwelling is essential for the individual and the family as well, and therefore should not be the property of another. A person living in another person's house in return for rent, or even without rent, is not a free person, and attempts made by countries to solve the housing problem have not provided a definitive solution. This is because such attempts did not target the ultimate solution: that a person must own his own home. Instead those endeavours dealt with the issue of rent either by reducing, increasing its value or standardizing the system by legislation, regardless of whether the landlord is the state or a private individual.

In a socialist society, it is inadmissible for anyone to control the needs of a human being, not even society itself. No one has the right to build a house in addition to his own dwelling, or the dwellings of his heirs, for the purpose of leasing it to others, because a house represents a human need. To build an additional house with the intention of leasing it is to engage in manipulating the need of another human being, and freedom lies at the very heart of human needs.

Income

Income is an imperative need for every human being, and as such, it is inadmissible that any member of society should obtain his or her income either as a wage from any source or as a charitable donation from any individual or party. In a socialist society there are no wage earners but only partners. One's income is a private matter to be dispensed personally, and within the limits of fulfilling personal needs. This income may be in the form of a share in a product in whose production a person constitutes an essential element. It should not be in the form of a wage received in return for production for the benefit of any other party whatsoever.

Vehicles

A vehicle is also an essential need for the individual and the family, and as such, a person's means of transportation should not be the property of another. In a socialist society no person or party may own private means of transportation for the purpose of renting to others, because this represents controlling the needs of others.

Land

Land is no one's private property. Rather, everyone has the right to exploit it for farming or grazing, for the duration of his or her life and the lives of their heirs, but within the limits of fulfilling their needs. If it

> *Land is no one's private property.*

were permissible for land to be privately owned, only those living would have a share of it. This is because while land is permanent, those who benefit from the land undergo, with the passage of time, changes in their jobs, their abilities and their lives too.

The objective of the new socialist society is to establish a happy society deriving its happiness from being free. Such a society is realized only through the fulfilment of the individual's spiritual and material needs, and this can be achieved by liberating these needs from the control and manipulation of others. Satisfaction of needs should be realized without exploitation or enslavement of others, as this would be contrary to the objectives of the new socialist society.

Thus in this new society, a human being should either work for himself to secure his material needs, or work for a collectively-owned establishment in which he is a partner sharing in its production, or join the public service to serve society, which in return would guarantee to provide for his material needs.

Economic activity in the new socialist society is a productive one for the satisfaction of material needs. It is not an unproductive activity nor one that seeks profit for the purpose of accumulating savings beyond what is needed to meet those material needs. Such an objective would be inconceivable under the new socialist rules. The legitimate objective of an individual's economic activity is solely the fulfilment of personal material needs, since the wealth of our world, as well as that of each individual society, is finite at every stage. No one individual has the right to undertake an economic activity, whereby wealth exceeding his needs can be amassed. The excess would represent the right of others. The individual has the right to save from his needs, from his own production only, but not from the efforts of others, or at the expense of their needs. If it were permissible to pursue economic activities for the purpose of making profit in excess of personal needs, some individuals would obtain more than they need and would then deprive others from obtaining their own needs. Savings in excess of personal needs represent another person's share of the wealth of society. To allow private production to secure savings in excess of satisfying personal needs, and to permit the employment of others to secure personal needs or to obtain in excess of personal needs, is the very essence of exploitation.

> The legitimate objective of the individuals' economic activity is solely the fulfilment of their material needs.

As we previously noted, labour in return for wages is virtually the same as enslaving a human being: it is unmotivated labour because the producer is a hired hand and not a partner. He who labours for himself is undoubtedly sincere in his productive work because dependence on one's own toil to fulfil one's own natural needs, prompts sincerity. Similarly, he who works in a socialist establishment is undoubtedly sincere in his productive work, because he is entitled to a share in production which secures his personal need and this also prompts his sincerity. But he who labours for a wage lacks the motivation to work. The system of wage earners cannot resolve the problem of increased and improved productivity in goods or services, and productivity continuously deteriorates because it is performed by unmotivated wage earners.

The following are examples of paid labour for the benefit of society; paid labour for the benefit of a private employer; and labour without pay.

First example

a) A labourer produces 10 apples for the benefit of society. The society offers him one apple in return for his labour and this apple completely satisfies his needs.

b) A labourer produces 10 apples for the benefit of society. The society offers him one apple for his labour and this apple does not suffice for the satisfaction of his needs.

Second example

A labourer produces 10 apples for the benefit of another individual, and in return receives a wage that represents less than the price of one apple.

Third example

A labourer produces 10 apples for himself.

Conclusion

First example

a) The labourer will not increase his production because even if he does he will not personally earn more than one apple for his labour and this one apple suffices his needs. Thus, all the labour force working for society is psychologically unmotivated and automatically negligent.

b) The labourer lacks the incentive to produce because he is producing for society and is not receiving in return what he needs in return. But he continues to work without motivation because, like all other members of society, he is constrained to comply with the general working conditions prevailing in his society.

Second example

The labourer does not work to produce in the first place. He works to receive a wage, but since he receives less than what suffices his needs, this worker would either seek another employer to sell his labour to for a better price, or would be constrained to hold on to his job to survive.

Third example

This labourer is the only one who produces eagerly and voluntarily. In a socialist society it is inadmissible for an individual to receive more than what suffices his needs, in return for his productivity, nor is it admissible for an individual to fulfil personal needs at the expense of others, or through the labours of others. Socialist establishments operate in order to meet the needs of society, and this third example reflects the proper condition for economic production.

However, in all cases, even under deplorable conditions, production is an activity essential for survival. This is evident in capitalist societies where production expands and accumulates in the hands of the few who do not labour but exploit the labour of workers who are still forced to toil and produce for a living. However, *The Green Book* not only offers a solution to the problem of material production. It also shows the way towards a comprehensive solution of the problems facing human societies, so that individuals may ultimately be spiritually and materially liberated, so that their happiness may be realized.

Other examples: if we assume that the wealth of society amounts to 10 units and the population count is 10, then the share of one individual in this wealth is one-tenth of the total, one unit per person. If a number of these individuals were to own more than their share of one unit, then certain other individuals in this society would own nothing, because their shares of the society's wealth had been usurped by others. This disparity creates the presence of the rich and the poor in an exploitative society. Let us suppose that five individuals in this society own two units each, then there are five others who own nothing, and this means that half are deprived of their share of the wealth, because the additional units owned by each one of the former five individuals represent the shares of the other five.

When an individual in this society requires only one unit of society's wealth to fulfil his needs, then the individual who owns more than one unit of this wealth, is actually the usurper of the right of other individuals in society. By having a share in excess of his need, this individual is usurping this excess to hoard more than his share at the expense of other people's needs. This explains the existence of those who hoard and do not spend, i.e. those who save in excess of what they require to fulfil their needs, and also the existence of those who are deprived, i.e. those who are demanding their right in society's wealth and have nothing to live by. It is overt theft and plunder, but is considered legitimate by the unjust and exploitative rules that govern such a society.

What is left over after fulfilling the needs of all individuals becomes the rightful property of all members of society. As for individuals, they can save as much as they choose, provided that they do so by cutting down on their needs since amassing in excess of personal needs is a violation of the sanctity of public wealth. Even the industrious and skilful have no right to usurp the share of others as a result of this advantage. They can use these talents to satisfy their own needs and save from those needs. This does not mean that the aged and the mentally or physically disabled are not entitled to the same share of society's wealth as other sound individuals.

The wealth of a society may be likened to a provisions establishment or warehouse, which supplies a number of people on a daily basis with a specific quantity of provisions to meet their daily needs. An individual is free to save as much as he chooses from the quantity he receives, and would thus be profiting from his abilities and proficiency. But he who takes advantage of such talent to obtain for himself more than his share, is undoubtedly a thief. Whoever uses his proficiency to gain more than is required to fulfil his personal needs actually violates the public right, i.e. society's wealth.

In the new socialist society, inequality of wealth between individuals is unacceptable, except for public servants who are assigned a specific share of society's wealth commensurate with their

> *Inequality of wealth between individuals is unacceptable.*

productivity and the services they perform. The difference between the shares of these public servants is determined by the extent of services performed and level of productivity.

Thus, human experiences have finally yielded a new experiment in a unique attempt to culminate man's struggle for complete freedom and happiness, fulfilling his needs, breaking free from the shackles of exploitation, bringing an end to tyranny and finding the way to a just distribution of society's wealth: an individual must work to fulfil his own needs, and must refrain from exploiting others, or compromising their needs.

This new experience is based on the theory of the fulfilment of needs for the emancipation of man.

Thus the new socialist society is no more than a dialectical consequence of the unjust relations prevailing in the world. This new socialist society embodies

> *The fulfilment of needs leads to the emancipation of humanity.*

the natural solution which stipulates private ownership to fulfil personal needs without exploitation, and collective property whereby the producers are partners in the production, replacing private enterprise which is based on the production of others without recognizing their right for a just share of the product.

He who owns the house in which you live, the vehicle in which you ride, or the income on which you live, either completely or partially controls your freedom. Freedom is undividable. Freedom is an essential pre-requisite for achieving happiness, and to be free, a human being must personally own what he needs, since he who owns another person's necessities controls, exploits and may even enslave this person despite any legislation to the contrary.

The material needs of people that are first and foremost are clothing, food, home and personal means of transportation. These are sacrosanct and must be privately owned. They are not to be leased from others. To obtain these essential personal needs in return for payment is to enable the real owner to intervene in another person's private life and control his essential needs, even if this owner were society in general. As a result, man's liberty is manipulated and man's aspiration to happiness is aborted. The owner of your rented clothing may step in to divest you of your clothes leaving you stripped naked on the open road, the owner of your rented vehicle may also step in to reclaim his possession leaving you in the middle of the road, and the owner of the house may come over to demand his house rendering you homeless without shelter.

Man's essential needs cannot be regulated by legal or administrative measures. Instead, such needs should constitute the foundations of society, in accordance with natural rules.

> *The aim of a socialist society is the happiness of man.*

The aim of a socialist society is the happiness of man. This happiness cannot be realized except in conditions of spiritual and material freedom. However, the realization of freedom depends upon the extent to which man personally owns his essential needs and the extent to which such ownership is safeguarded.

The transformation of contemporary societies of wage earners into societies of partners is inevitable as a dialectical outcome of the contradictory economic theories prevailing in our world today, and as the inevitable dialectal result of the unresolved oppressive relationship originating from the wage system. The intimidating power of trade unions in the capitalist world is potentially capable of transforming capitalist wage-earning societies into societies of partners. The potential for revolution to establish socialism exists. It begins with an uprising of the producers to seize their share of the production they produce. The objectives of labour strikes shall change from demands for wage increases into demands for shares in production, and this shall be achieved sooner or later with the guidance of *The Green Book*. The final step in the process will be accomplished when the new socialist society reaches the stage whereby money and profit disappear as society becomes fully productive and the level of production reaches the point whereby it meets the material needs of all the members of the society. Profit automatically disappears at this final stage and the need for money as a medium of exchange no longer exists. The recognition of profit is an admission of exploitation, since the mere fact of recognition implies that the pursuit of profit knows no limits. Attempts to limit profit-making are merely reformist not radical and do not prevent the exploitation of man. Since profit is the motivating force of economic production, the abolition of profit as the final solution is not a matter of decision. It is a consequence of the development of a socialist production, and will be accomplished when this production fulfils the material needs of society and all its members. Work for the purpose of increasing profit finally leads to the disappearance of profit.

Domestic servants

A house should be serviced by its occupants.

Domestic servants – whether wage earners or otherwise – represent a condition of servitude; they are actually the slaves of our modern times. And since the new socialist society is based on partnership and not on a wage system, the natural socialist rules do not apply to house servants. They offer services not production, and services do not entail material production divisible into shares, as natural socialist rules stipulate. This is why domestic servants cannot work except in return for a wage or even without a wage in unfortunate circumstances. But being of a level lower than the level of wage labourers, house servants are more deserving of emancipation from the fetters of servitude in the society of wage earners, the society of slaves. Domestic servants are a social phenomenon second only to the phenomenon of slavery. The Third Universal Theory is a harbinger of the final deliverance of the masses from all the constraints of injustice, tyranny, exploitation, and political and economic subordination. It also heralds the advent of all people's society in which all individuals are free and equal in authority, wealth, and arms. Freedom may finally triumph.

The Green Book shows the way to the deliverance of the masses of wage earners and domestic servants, and to the realization of man's freedom. That is why there is no way other than the way of struggle to free domestic servants from their condition of servitude and remove them from the confines of houses, to transform them as partners in domains where material production is divisible into shares. Houses should be serviced by their occupants, and house chores should not be done by servants in return for wages or without wages, but by employed persons subject to promotion during their employment, and enjoying material and social benefits just like other public servants.

Part Three

The Social Basis of the Third
Universal Theory

The social factor i.e. the national, is the driving force of human history. This factor is the bond that binds together different human communities and which unites the family, the clan and the nation. It is the basic key in the progress of history.

Heroes in history are individuals who have made sacrifices for the sake of one cause or another. But what were those causes? They sacrificed themselves for the sake of others. But who are those others? They are those with whom there is a relationship binding them together. This relationship that binds an individual to his community is a social one. It is the relationship between members of a community, the national bond that constitutes the basic component in the make-up of a particular people or nation. Therefore social causes are invariably national in nature, and proceed from the national relationship. The term social derives from the notion of the group, and denotes the relationship between members of a given community. The term national derives from the notion of the nation, and denotes the relationship between members of a given people. As such, the social relationship is the national relationship, and the national relationship is the social relationship. Even if small in number, communities or groups form one nation regardless of the individual relationship amongst its members. The term community here is intended to denote the permanent community by virtue of the national ties that bind its members.

Historic movements are mass movements, i.e. the movement of one community for its own interests, independent of other communities. Mass movements are independent movements seeking to assert the identity of a community oppressed by another.

The struggle for authority is a phenomenon which occurs within a community, even at the level of the family, as explained in Part One of this book: "The

Political Basis of the Third Universal Theory". A group movement is a nation's movement for its own interests. Because of its national structure, each group has common social needs that must be collectively satisfied. These needs are not in any way individual needs; they are collective rights, demands, needs or objectives, required by a nation bound together by a single ethos. For this reason these movements are called national movements. Contemporary national liberation movements are also social movements, and shall not cease to occur until every group is liberated from the domination of another. The world today is passing through one of history's natural cycles: the social struggle in support of national identity.

It is a universal fact that national struggle – social struggle – is the primary driving force in the movement of history; it is the essential factor, the fundamental factor, and therefore the strongest of all other factors. In the world of mankind, this is both the historical reality as it is the social reality. This driving force is part of the nature of nations and human communities, even of life itself. Animals other than humans live together in groups because a community is the basis for the survival of species in the animal kingdom. Similarly, the existence of a national identity is the basis for the survival of nations.

Those nations whose national identity has been destroyed are nations whose very existence has been destroyed. Minorities, one of the world's main political problems, are caused by a social factor. They are nations whose national identity has been destroyed and which are thus torn apart. The social factor, essential to life, is therefore also a factor of survival. It is the nation's innate driving force as it strives to survive.

The existence of a national identity in the world of mankind and group instinct in the animal kingdom are comparable to the force of gravity in the mineral kingdom and the domain of celestial bodies. If the sun were to be destroyed, gases would be released and – fundamental to its survival as a planet – its unity would no longer exist. Accordingly, the survival of an object depends on the unifying factor that maintains its cohesion. Similarly, the survival of a community depends on the unifying social factor, namely the existence of a national identity, and this is the driving force behind the struggle of communities to achieve their own national unity and to ensure their survival.

The national factor, the social bond, functions spontaneously to drive a nation to strive for survival, in the same way that the gravity of an object works to sustain the cohesion of an object as one mass collected around its nucleus or central part. In the theory of the atomic bomb, atomic diffusion results from the explosion of the nucleus, the source of gravity that sustains the mass around the atom. When this unifying element is destroyed, the gravitational pull is lost and all atoms are diffused and the bomb explodes away into particles releasing the powerful destructive energy. This is the nature of matter. Life is undermined if this confirmed natural law were to be disregarded or opposed. Similarly, an individual's life is undermined once the national bond, the social bond, is disregarded or opposed, for it is the gravitational pull of the group that is the secret of its survival. Except for the religious factor, there is no other factor that matches the social factor in the influence it exerts on the unity of a particular community. Religion may divide a nation and may also unite communities of diverse nationalities. Nevertheless, it is the social factor that finally prevails. This has been the case throughout the ages. Harmony should prevail when each nation belongs to one religion. However in reality this does not happen and it is diversity that prevails. This diversity has become the real cause of conflict and instability in the lives of the people in all times past and present.

A sound rule is that every nation should have a religion. Any contrary condition is an exception to this rule. Such an exception creates abnormal conditions that become a real cause for the eruption of conflicts within the communities of one national group. This problem cannot be resolved except by following the natural rule which stipulates that every nation should have a religion so that the social factor concurs with religious factor to create harmony, stabilize and strengthen the life of the communities and ensure their sound development.

Every nation should have a religion

Marriage may have a positive or a negative effect on the social factor. It is true that men and women are naturally free to accept or reject a proposed partner in marriage for whatever reason; nevertheless, taking partners from the same community naturally reinforces the cohesion of the community and promotes collective development in conformity with the social factor.

The family

To the individual, the family is more important than the state. Humanity recognizes the individual as a human being, and the normal individual acknowledges the family, which is his cradle, his origin and which serves as his social umbrella. Unlike the state, the individual and the family are natural entities. The human race has neither relations nor anything else to do with the state, which is an artificial, political, economic and sometimes military system. The family is precisely like a plant: made up of twigs and leaves and blossoms. Cultivating the natural environment into farms and gardens and the like, is an artificial accomplishment that has nothing to do with the nature of the plant.

The fact that certain political, economic or even military factors tie a number of families in one given state does not in any way link this system with humanity. Therefore, any measure, condition, or circumstance, which throws a family into disorder or leads to its dispersion and ruin is inhuman and goes against nature; it is oppressive and quite similar to an action, a circumstance or measure, which causes a plant to wither or perish, or which destroys its twigs, leaves and blossoms.

Societies, in which family unity and entity are threatened due to certain conditions, are analogous to a field in which plants are threatened by erosion, fire, drought, heat or aridity. A blossoming garden or field is that whose plants grow naturally, blossom, pollinate and take root. The same holds true of the human society.

A thriving society is one in which the family flourishes and the individual grows normally within its bosom, and is established as a member of the human community. But just as the leaf of a branch or the branch of a tree, if severed, loses its value and physical life, an individual severed from his family, i.e. an individual without a family, has no value or no social life. If the human community were ever to become a society without families, it would then become a community of tramps without roots, like artificial plants.

The tribe

The tribe is an extended family that has grown as a result of procreation. The tribe is in effect a large extended family, and it then follows that the nation is the tribe that has also grown as a result of procreation. The nation is a large extended tribe; and the world is the nation that has diversified into a multitude of nations. The world therefore is an enlarged nation.

The relationship that binds a family together is that same relationship which binds the tribe together, the nation and the world. Nevertheless, the larger the multitude of people the weaker this bond becomes. The essence of humanity is the national bond or nationalism, the essence of nationalism is belonging to a tribe, and the essence of belonging to a tribe is the familial bond. The warmth in this relationship gradually decreases in strength proportionally as it increases in size from the family entity up to the national entity. This is a sociological fact, denied only by the ignorant.

The social bond, cohesion, unity, familiarity and affection are all stronger at the familial level than at the tribal level, they are also stronger at the tribal level than at the national level, and are least strong at the universal level.

The benefits, advantages, values and ideals based on these social bonds exist where these bonds are natural and strong. They are in fact stronger at the family level than at the tribal level, and stronger on the tribal level than on the national level, and are least strong at the universal level. Thus, the social bonds, benefits, advantages and ideals associated with them gradually fade away, whenever the family, tribe, nation and human-kind become weaker or disappear.

This is why it is very important for the human community to preserve the cohesion of the family, the tribe, the nation and the world, in order to profit from the advantages, benefits, values and ideals yielded by the solidarity, cohesion, unity, familiarity and love of the family, tribe, nation and humanity.

Socially, the family is better than the tribal society, and the tribal society is better than the national society, which in turn is better than the world society in terms of kinship, compassion, solidarity and advantage.

The advantages of the tribe

As the tribe is a large extended family, the tribe provides its members with the natural benefits and social advantages that the family provides for its members, for the tribe is a secondary family. It is worth mentioning here that an individual may sometimes behave in a dishonourable manner that a family will not condone; yet because the family is relatively small in size, this individual will not be aware of its supervision. In contrast, individuals as members of a tribe cannot be free of its watchful eyes.

The code of ethics enforced by the tribe on its members is a kind of social education better and nobler than any school education. The tribe is actually a social school which people belong to from childhood, and are raised with ideals that take root and instinctively influence their behaviour in life as they grow older. Education and knowledge formally taught in schools gradually recede as individuals grow older, because they are aware that it was formal and compulsory, and because they are aware that they have been indoctrinated.

As a natural social "umbrella" for social security, the tribe, pursuant to its social tribal conditions, provides its members with collective protection and security in addition to collective reparations and collective compensation for bodily injury and revenge. The blood tie is the prime factor in the formation of the tribe, but affiliation is also one of its components. Over time the differences between the two components recede, leaving the tribe as a single social and physical unit, though it remains fundamentally a unit of blood and descent more any other.

The nation

A nation is the national political "umbrella" for individuals; it is far wider than the social "umbrella" provided by a tribe for its members. Tribalism undermines national identity because tribal loyalty weakens national loyalty and is maintained at its expense. In the same way, family loyalty weakens tribal loyalty and is maintained at its expense. And in so much as nationalist fanaticism is essential to a nation, it is at the same time a threat to humanity.

A nation in the international community is similar to a family in the tribe. The more partisan sentiments and internecine feuds afflict families of a single tribe, the more threatened the tribe becomes. A family is also threatened when its individual members feud and pursue only their personal interests. Similarly a nation is also threatened if partisan sentiments and internecine feuds erupt among its tribes. Nationalist fanaticism and the use of national force against a weaker nation, or national prosperity attained by a nation as result of overpowering another, is evil and detrimental to humanity. However, a strong individual, aware of his own responsibilities is important and an advantage to his family; a solid, self-respecting family, aware of its significance, is socially and materially an advantage to the tribe; and the civilized, well-advanced and productive nation, is in turn, beneficial to the whole world. Nevertheless, the national and political structure is corrupted if it were to stoop down to the social level, i.e. the familial and tribal levels, to interact with, and be influenced by their particular considerations.

A nation is a large extended family that passed through the tribal stage – the tribe, then a plurality of tribes, that have branched out from one common source. It also includes members who affiliated themselves with its destiny. The family likewise grows into a nation after going through the tribal stage from which it branches out into a further stage, the melting pot of commingling between various communities in society. This is a very slow but inevitable social evolution. Nevertheless, as new nations emerge with the passage of time, so old nations disintegrate. Common origin and common destiny, through affiliation, are the two historic bases for of any nation, though origin is the primary and affiliation comes second. A nation is not only an entity defined by its origin. It is also an entity that evolved from the accumulation of historical human activity to become the homeland for the multitudes who make its particular history, singular heritage and face a common destiny. Therefore, regardless of the blood tie, a nation, in the final analysis, is formed through a sense of belonging and a shared destiny.

But why has the world map witnessed the emergence and disappearance of great powers and the emergence and disappearance of other states? Is the reason political and unrelated to the social cornerstone of the Third Universal Theory or is it social and therefore relevant to the concerns of this part of *The Green Book*?

Let us see. The fact that the family is a social and not political entity is an irrefutable truth. The tribe too is a social entity because it was originally a family that procreated and multiplied into subdivisions, then expanded into clans, which eventually transformed into many other tribes. As such, a nation is a social entity whose people are bound by national identity, and the tribe is a social entity whose members are bound by tribal ties, and the family is also a social entity whose members are bound by familial bonds, and the nations of the world constitute a social entity bound by the bonds of humanity. These facts are all self-evident. There is then the political structure of states that form the political map of the world. But why should changes occur in this world map from one era to another? The reason has to do with the political structure and whether or not it conforms to the social structure of the state. When the political structure is in conformity with the social structure of a nation it endures and does not change. When it changes or declines as a result of colonial domination it re-emerges eventually as a result of national struggle, national awakening or national unity. When a political structure comprises more than one nation then the map of the state is ripped apart as each nation obtains its separate national independence. Such was the fate of past empires because they were comprised of many nations that were awakened and driven by nationalist sentiments to demand their independence. Thus political empires were ripped apart, and the nations reverted to their original social structures. The evidence is clearly there for examination through history.

But why are empires formed of several nations? The answer to this is found in the structure of the state that is not a social structure like the family, the tribe or the nation. Rather the state is a political entity created by several factors, the simplest and foremost of which is national identity. The national state is the only political structure in keeping with the natural social structure. Moreover, it is this state that endures, unless it is subjected to the tyranny of another more powerful nation, or its political structure as a state is affected by its social structure in the form of tribes, clans or families. When subjected to and influenced by a familial, tribal or sectarian social structure, the political formation of the state becomes corrupted.

Religious, economic and military factors also contribute to form a state that differs from the basic national state. A common religion may create a state that embraces several nations. Economic imperatives and military conquests may do the same. Thus the world can witness the existence of a state or empire in one particular historical period, but then witnesses its fall and disappearance in another. When the spirit of nationalism is more powerful than the religious spirit, conflict intensifies among the various nationalities bound by the ties of one religion. Such conflicts eventually culminate in the independence of each nation that reverts to its own social structure and the empire finally disappears. Religion resurfaces when the religious spirit emerges stronger than the spirit of nationalism. Consequently the various nationalities eventually unite under the banner of religion until the time when once again the national factor again overrides the religious factor.

All states made up of diverse nationalities for religious, economic, military or ideological reasons shall eventually be ripped apart by national conflict until every nationality gains its independence. The social factor will inevitably triumph over the political factor.

Despite the political imperatives which necessitate the establishment of the state, the family remains first and foremost the basis of the life of individuals extending then to the tribe, then the nation and finally, to all humanity. The social factor is the basic and constant factor. It is imperative to concentrate on the social reality by first attending to the

> The family is first and foremost the basis of the life of individuals.

family in order that the normal, well-bred individual may emerge, then moving on to the tribe, as a "social umbrella" and a natural social school which further educates the individual raised by his family, and finally, to the nation. This plan is necessary as it stems from the need for individuals to learn the worth of social values from both family and tribe, the two naturally formed social structures which evolve without the deliberate interference of man. The social factor, i.e. the national factor, is the real and constant driving force of history.

To disregard the social bond of human communities, and to establish a political system counter to social reality is to create a temporary structure which will collapse because of the movement of the social factor i.e. the national.

These are not interpretations of concepts; they are all facts in the life of mankind. Every individual should recognize these so that his or her actions may be worthwhile. To avoid deviation, disorder and corruption in the life of human groups that are a result of lack of understanding and respect of the principles of human life, it is essential to know these confirmed truths.

Women

Women, like men, are human beings. This is an incontestable truth. Therefore as humans, it is a fact that women are equal to men and to discriminate between them is a glaring inexcusable injustice. Like men, women eat and drink, love and hate. They can equally think, learn and comprehend, and they equally need shelter, clothing and means of transportation, and just like men, they feel the bite of hunger and thirst, and they also live and die.

But why are there men and women? Human community is not made up solely of men or women; it is naturally both sexes. Why is it then that both sexes were created? Why didn't creation exclude one of the two? Why was it decreed that both sexes come into being? The existence of both men and women implies that there is a natural necessity for the existence of both, rather than man only or woman only. It follows then that each is not exactly like the other, and therefore, there is a natural difference between man and woman. This in turn signifies an assigned role for each that differs in accordance with the difference between the two sexes. Each is to have his or her own prevailing conditions in order that they might live and perform their assigned roles.

In order to understand this role we must understand the natural difference between the two sexes. Women are female and men are male. According to gynaecologists women, unlike men, menstruate each month. This menstrual cycle is a natural ailment that women must experience every month; if they cannot experience this, they are barren. When a woman becomes pregnant, due to her pregnancy, she becomes less active for about a year because her pregnancy inhibits her natural vitality until she delivers the baby. After delivery or miscarriage, a woman is in a state of confinement. Since men cannot be impregnated they do not experience the ailments that women do. Afterwards, a woman nurses the infant she gave birth to. She breastfeeds for nearly two years, and this means that mother and child are necessarily inseparable for the duration of nursing. Hence, the woman whose activity has already been diminished is also directly responsible for another human being who needs to be aided with all his biological functions, or else will not survive. Men are naturally exempt from all this.

These natural characteristics form the essential differences between women and men. They illustrate the essential necessity for the existence of both male and female. Each sex has its own particular life role or function and these are different and irreplaceable – neither can ever assume the function of the other. In this context, it should be noted that these biological functions constitute a heavy burden on women and cost them a considerable amount of effort and pain. Nevertheless, human life would cease without these female functions which are neither mandatory nor optional but simply essential, and without which human life would cease altogether.

Deliberate interventions against conception constitute an alternative to human life. Also there exists partial deliberate intervention against conception, as well as against breastfeeding. All these are links in a chain of actions in contradiction to natural life, the ultimate of which is murder as when a woman kills herself to avoid pregnancy, to avoid giving birth and breastfeeding. Although they vary in degree, these are not unlike other artificial interventions employed against the natural processes of life such as pregnancy and breastfeeding, marriage and motherhood.

Dispensing with the normal function of the woman as a mother by allowing day nurseries to replace the mother's care, is the first step towards dispensing with the human society and turning it into a merely biological society with an artificial way of life. To separate children from their mothers and cram them in nurseries is to treat them just like chicks in chicken coops, and it is only natural motherhood that is appropriate and right for the children of mankind. Children are to grow up in a family where motherhood, fatherhood and comradeship of brothers and sisters prevail and not in an institution resembling a poultry farm. Clearly, poultry need a mother's care at certain stages, just like the rest of the young in the animal kingdom. Breeding these birds on farms, which are in a way similar to nurseries, is counterproductive to their normal growth. Their meat is more like processed meat; they are not tasty and may not even be nutritious because they do not grow naturally. As for children who are orphans and homeless, society is their guardian. Only for them should society establish nurseries, orphanages and the like to accommodate them. They are better off as charges of society than as charges of individuals who are not their natural parents.

If a test were carried out to discover the natural propensity of a child, the child would choose his mother rather than the nursery. As a child is naturally disposed towards his mother, the mother is the natural and proper person to give the child the protection of nursing. Placing a child in a day nursery, is coercive and tyrannical and a violation of the child's free and natural disposition.

Placing a child in a day nursery is coercion and a violation of the child's free and natural disposition.

Natural growth for all living things is free and healthy growth. To substitute a nursery for a mother is a coercion that runs counter to the freedom of proper growth. Children who are shipped off to nurseries are led with compulsion as gullible simple-minded babies, and for purely material reasons rather than compelling social reasons. Without the constraints and the gullibility of innocence, children would choose to stay close to their mothers and reject nurseries as an abnormal and inhuman alternative. The only justification for such an unnatural and inhuman process is the fact that the woman is in a position unsuitable to her natural role; she is required to perform duties other than social obligations, which are in conflict with the duties of motherhood.

A woman, to whom nature assigned a natural role other than that assigned to men, must be in an appropriate position to perform her natural role.

Motherhood is the female's function, not the male's. Consequently it is in the natural order that children should not be separated from their mothers, and any measure taken to do so is tyrannical, oppressive and dictatorial. Also, any mother who forsakes her duties towards her children goes against her natural role in life. A woman should not be subjected to tyranny and oppression, and should be given rights and provided with adequate conditions which would allow her to perform her natural role in normal conditions. The contradiction arises when necessity obliges women to forsake their natural function of childbearing and motherhood. This necessity indicates that they are subject to oppression and dictatorial treatment, since a woman in need of work, which would restrict her ability to perform her natural function, is not free and is compelled to work by need and in need no freedom indeed.

To perform their natural female function, women need the conditions appropriate to an ailing person overburdened by pregnancy, bearing the load of another human life, and thus physically unable to perform other roles with efficiency. It is unfair for a woman passing through this stage of motherhood, to be placed in a situation that disagrees with her pregnant condition, i.e. to be required to exert physical effort. This would be tantamount to a punishment inflicted upon her for her betrayal of her maternal role; it is a tax imposed on her for entering the realm of men, which is naturally alien to their own.

Those who believe that women voluntarily perform work that requires physical effort are in error. The grim reality indicates otherwise. They do such work because they were unwittingly led by the merciless materialistic society into compelling circumstances in which they have no alternative but to yield to social conditions in the mistaken belief that they are working of their own free will. In fact the alleged basis that maintains that women and men are in every respect not different from each other, deprives the woman of her freedom.

The phase "in every respect" is the grand deception that ensnares women. This idea destroys the appropriate and necessary conditions that women need and are unquestionably entitled to, to the exclusion of men by virtue of their distinctive natural role in life.

To consider women capable of carrying equal burdens as men while pregnant is unjust and cruel; and to consider them as capable in times of hardship and fasting while breastfeeding is equally unjust and cruel. It is even more so if they are considered capable of doing a disagreeable job that disgraces and taints their femininity. It is also equally unjust and cruel to have women study a discipline that would lead them to jobs incompatible with their nature. However, there is no difference whatsoever between men and women as human beings. Both are not to be forced into marrying against their will and both are not to be divorced without the due process of law or without mutual agreement outside the courtroom, or even to be married without prior agreement on divorce. Moreover, the woman is the rightful owner of the house, because a home is necessary to women who become pregnant, who give birth, experience confinement and perform the duties of motherhood. Even in the world of other animals, the female whose natural duty is motherhood is the rightful owner of her home – the shelter of motherhood. It would thus be unjust to deprive children of their mother and to deprive mothers of their homes.

The different biological nature of females bestows upon women characteristics different from those of men, in both form and intrinsic nature. Women are different from men in form because they are females, just as all females in the kingdoms of plants and animals, differ from the males of their species. This is an undisputable fact of nature. The male in the plant and animal kingdoms is born naturally strong and striving, while the female in both kingdoms is naturally born beautiful and gentle. According to these diverse characteristics and the laws of nature, the male voluntarily performs the role of the strong, striving being because he was born as such, while the female performed the role of the beautiful gentle being spontaneously, because she was born as such. This natural rule is just: on the one hand, because it is natural, and on the other, because it is the basic rule for freedom. All living things are created free, and any interference with this freedom is coercion. When these natural rules are breached or scorned, the values of life itself are abused and corrupted. Nature has been so designed so as to be in harmony with the inevitability of life from what is being to what will become. When a creature is born to life it is a living being and shall inevitably be so until it dies. Survival between the beginning and the end is thus based on the natural law of creation, a state of neither compulsion nor choice, just nature taking its course; it is natural freedom.

In the worlds of man, animals and plants, there must be both sexes, for life to occur and to proceed on its course from being to non-being. This does not happen by the mere existence of male and female, but by the fully efficient performance of the natural roles for which they were created. If this does not happen the course of life is impaired for one reason or another. This is the present state of societies almost everywhere in the world, as a result of the roles of men and women becoming confused by the attempts to transform women into men. In harmony with their particular nature and its purpose, men and women must excel themselves in the roles naturally assigned to them. To resist this situation is regression, a course that goes against nature and destroys the basis of freedom, for it is hostile to both life and survival. Men and women must relentlessly adhere to the role he or she was created for. Abandoning this role implies compelling circumstances that in turn, imply an abnormal situation. The woman who refrains from childbearing, marriage and motherhood, and who forsakes her gentleness and dismisses adornment for health reasons is a woman who relinquishes her natural role in life, because of these compelling health conditions. The woman who refrains from childbearing, marriage or motherhood in favour of work also relinquishes her natural role in life because of compelling circumstances. The woman who abstains from one or all these functions for no substantive reasons, relinquishes her natural role in life because of compelling and morally deviant circumstances. Thus, abandoning his or her natural role in life for a male or female is an indication that he or she is subjected to abnormal circumstances, opposed to freedom and are a threat to survival. Therefore, a world revolution is needed to do away with all the materialistic conditions that prevent women from performing their natural role in life and so drives them to carry out men's duties in order to achieve equal rights. Such a revolution is inevitable, especially in industrial societies. It is a reaction

> *Therefore a world revolution is needed to do away with all the materialistic conditions that hinder a women from performing their natural role in life.*

to the instinct of survival, even without any instigator of revolution, not even from *The Green Book*.

All societies today look upon women as little more than commodities. In the East she is looked upon as a personal possession to be bought and sold, and in the West her femininity is not recognized.

Driving a woman to do a man's work is an unfair aggression against the femininity that is naturally bestowed upon her for a natural purpose essential to life. Man's work obliterates the beautiful features which creation awarded to women so that they might perform their particular role. It is just like flowers that need to attract pollinators to produce seeds. The role of plants in life would come to an end if we were to obliterate flowers, and it is the same with butterflies, birds and other female animals that are colourfully adorned for this vital natural purpose. To undertake man's work, women must abandon their role and beauty and become men. A woman has full rights and need not be coerced to turn into a man and forsake her femininity.

> A woman has full rights and need not be coerced to turn into a man and forsake her femininity.

There is a natural difference between men and women resulting from the difference in the physical constitution between the two sexes that gives female organs functions different from those of male organs. There is also a difference in disposition, nature, temperament and shape of body. A woman is beautiful, compassionate and emotional. She is easily frightened and is generally a gentle being, while a man is aggressive by virtue of his inbred nature.

It is absolutely uncivilized to ignore these natural differences between men and women. It is against the laws of nature, is destructive to human life, and is a real cause of the wretchedness of human social life.

In the industrial societies of our time, women have adapted themselves in order to perform masculine physical work, at the expense of their femininity and natural function in life, and to the detriment of their beauty, mind and duties of motherhood. It would be stupid, even dangerous to civilization and humanity to imitate such materialistic and uncivilized societies.

This is not a question of whether women should or should not work. It is ridiculous to pose the problem as such. Work and opportunities should be made available by society to all capable and needy individuals, women and men, provided that each individual works in an appropriate domain and is not coerced by oppressive circumstances to go into inappropriate domains. To have children working in adult domains is dictatorial and an outrage, and to have women working in the domain of masculine work is similarly dictatorial and an outrage.

Hence, freedom is to have an individual learn an appropriate discipline to qualify for work befitting to himself, and dictatorship is to have an individual learn an inappropriate discipline and thus be driven to do work unbefitting to himself. Work that befits a man is not always work appropriate for a woman, and knowledge that is suitable for adults is not the knowledge suitable for children.

There is no difference in human rights between men and women or between adults and children. Yet there is no full equality in terms of their duties.

> *There is no difference in human rights between a man and a woman; rather it is their roles and duties which differ.*

Minorities

What is a minority? What are the rights and respons-ibilities of a minority? How can the problem of minorities be resolved according to the solution to the various problems of humanity presented by the Third Universal Theory?

Minorities are of two kinds only: a minority belonging to a nation, and its nation provides it with its social framework; and a minority that has no nation and thus, forms its own social framework. The latter makes historical contributions that accumulate and eventually create a nation by virtue of belonging and destiny.

This minority has its own social rights as we have seen, and it would be unjust of any party or majority to infringe upon these rights. The social characteristics particular to a minority are not transferable or divestible. The political and economic problems of minorities can only be solved within a society controlled by the masses where power, wealth and weapons are in the hands of the people. To look upon a minority as a political and economic minority is dictatorial and unjust.

Black people

Black people will prevail in the world.

The last period in history that has known slavery was that which witnessed the white man enslaving the black race. This period shall remain vivid in the minds of the black people until they regain their self-respect.

This tragic historical phenomenon that is painful to remember, and the black people's psychological search for a satisfactory way to deal with this past and to regain self-respect, is a psychological incentive that cannot be disregarded in the movement of the black race to avenge itself and triumph. In addition, there are inevitable cycles of social history: the yellow race's domination of the world, when it came from Asia, and the white race's attempts at colonizing extensive areas of all continents of the world. Now, it is the turn of the black race to re-emerge.

The black race is at present in a dire and backward social condition. This backwardness is working in the interest of the numerical superiority of this race. Their low standard of living has rendered these people immune from knowledge of methods of birth control and its regulation. Their backward social traditions are responsible for the absence of restrictions in marriage leading to an unchecked and high birth rate. This is at a time when other races are diminishing in number as a result of the practice of birth control and other restrictions in the laws of marriage, as well as a preoccupation with work; this is in contrast to the black people whose lassitude is due to living in constantly hot climate.

Learning

Learning and teaching must not merely involve regular syllabuses and specific materials that young people are constrained to learn during specified hours, using printed books and copybooks. This kind of education that prevails throughout the world today is against freedom. Mandatory education which countries of the world are proud to enforce on their youth is a coercive education that suppresses freedom. It forcibly stunts human talents and forcibly directs human choice. It is tyrannical and destroys freedom because it deprives human beings of free choice, and hinders brilliance and creativity. To force a human being to learn a particular curriculum is dictatorial. To impose specific teaching materials is a dictatorial act.

> *To force a human being to learn a particular curriculum is dictatorial.*

Mandatory learning and regular systematic teaching are in reality a forced stultification of the masses. All countries that determine teaching courses through the implementation of formal curriculums, imposed on their people, formally determining the material and knowledge to be taught, are countries that oppress their citizens. A worldwide cultural revolution must destroy all the prevalent educational systems in the world to liberate the human mentality from syllabuses that nurture fanaticism and the deliberate reshaping of man's concepts, his tastes and mentality.

This is not – as it may seem to superficial readers – a call to close down educational institutions. Nor is it an invitation to people to shun education. On the contrary, it is a call for society to provide all kinds of education and give the people the freedom of selecting the discipline of their choice. Educational institutions need the capacity to provide all branches of knowledge; otherwise man's liberty is restricted and he will be forced to learn only the disciplines available and thus be deprived of his natural right. Societies that restrict knowledge or monopolize knowledge are reactionary, and ardent adherents of ignorance as well as being hostile to freedom. Societies that monopolize religious knowledge are also reactionary, ardent adherents of ignorance and hostile to freedom. Likewise societies that distort the religions, civilizations and behaviour of others in the process of teaching those subjects, are also fanatic, reactionary and hostile to freedom. Societies that prohibit materialistic knowledge are likewise reactionary societies, biased towards ignorance and hostile to freedom. Knowledge is a natural right for every human being and no one has the right to deprive others of knowledge, unless a person has committed an act that deprives him or her of that right.

Ignorance will come to an end when everything is presented as it really is; it will end when knowledge about everything is made available to every human being in a suitable way.

> *Ignorance will come to an end when everything is presented as it really is.*

Music and art

Humans, being backward, are still unable to express themselves in one common language. Until this human aspiration is realized, which seems impossible, all expressions of joy and sorrow, good and evil, beauty and ugliness, comfort and distress, annihilation and immortality, love and hate, as well as expressions of colours, feelings, tastes and disposition, shall all be expressed in the language spoken spontaneously by each person. Behaviour will result from the reaction to the sense that the language creates in he speaker's mind.

To learn one language, whatever this language is, is not the solution at present. This problem shall remain unresolved until the process of unifying languages runs its course through time, provided that the hereditary factor loses its effect on subsequent generations. Ancestral and parental feelings, tastes and dispositions, meld the feelings, tastes and dispositions of children and grandchildren. If those ancestors spoke several languages to express themselves, and on the contrary their children spoke only one language to express themselves, their offspring would not necessarily share the same tastes even though they speak a common language. The unification of taste is only achieved when the new language melds together the tastes and feelings inherited from one generation to another.

If a community of people wears white on a mournful occasion and another dresses in black, then each community develops particular attitudes towards these colours; one community would like white and dislike black and the other would like black and dislike white. Moreover, this attitude leaves a physical effect on the cells as well as on the genes in the body. This adaptation will be transmitted by inheritance, and the heir would come to dislike the colour disliked by his parents, as a result of inheriting their feelings. Consequently people only relate to their own arts and heritage. Due to the factor of heredity, this feeling of harmony eludes them when they come into contact with the arts of others who differ in heritage and yet speak a single common language.

Such a difference emerges among communities of one people, even if only on a small scale.

Learning one language is not the problem, and understanding the arts of others as result of learning their language is not the problem either. The problem lies in the impossibility of genuine mental adaptation to another people's language. This shall remain impossible until the time when traces of heredity vanish from the body of the human being.

Mankind is still backward because humans do not yet communicate in one inherited common language. It is only a matter of time before we reach this goal, unless civilization should suffer a relapse.

Sports, horsemanship and the stage

Sport is either private, like praying performed by a person alone in the privacy of a closed room, or public practiced collectively in fields and arenas, like praying collectively in places of worship. Public sport is what interests all people. They practice these sports and do not let others practice it in their stead, since this is as inconceivable as having a crowd enter a place of worship to watch one or more worshippers praying, without praying themselves! It is also inconceivable for crowds to enter athletic fields and stadiums to watch one or more players, without practicing the games themselves.

Sports are like praying, eating, and like the comfort of warmth and coolness. It would be foolish for a crowd to enter a restaurant to watch one or more persons eating, or to let one or more persons enjoy warming their bodies in their place. It is unacceptable for a society to permit an individual or a team to monopolize sports to the exclusion of other members of society. Neither is it acceptable for society to bear the expenses of such a monopoly by one individual or team. This is as an unacceptable as having a people democratically allowing an individual, or a group – whether a party, a social class, a sect, a tribe or an assembly – to determine their destiny on their behalf or determine their needs for them.

Privately practiced sport is of no interest to anyone except the person who exercises on his own and at his own expense. However public sports are a common need for people and no one person, or group of persons, can play a game of sports on behalf of the people, neither from the physical nor from the democratic point of view. Physically speaking, this representative player cannot transmit to others what physical benefits he gained from the exercise; and democratically speaking, no individual or team has the right to monopolize sports, power, wealth or weapons, to the exclusion of others.

Sporting clubs which constitute the traditional sports institutions in the world today and are maintained by public funds and other public means of support in every country, are rapacious social instruments, not unlike the dictatorial political instruments which monopolize power to the exclusion of the people, and the economic instruments which monopolize society's wealth, as well as the traditional military instruments which monopolize weapons, acting as substitutes for society.

The era of the masses that destroys the monopolizing instruments of wealth, power and weapons, shall inevitably destroy the instruments that monopolize social activities such as sports and horsemanship. The masses line up to support a candidate to act as their representative in determining their destiny on the impossible assumption that this candidate shall represent them and uphold their dignity and sovereignty and all related considerations, and are eventually alienated, as they watch a person doing what they should naturally be doing themselves. These same masses are like the crowds that do not play sports themselves, due to their inability to do so because of their ignorance and because they are scorned by the monopolizing instruments that are bent on distracting these numbed crowds that laugh and applaud instead of practicing the sport monopolized by these rapacious instruments.

Sport should be for the masses.

Sport, like power, should be for the masses, and just as wealth and weapons should be for the people, sport as a social activity should also be for the people.

Public sport is for all the people. It is the right of all because in addition to entertainment, it is beneficial to health. It is unreasonable to let sport be monopolized by particular groups who obtain its moral and health benefits to the exclusion of others, while the masses offer public sport all the needed facilities and means of support, and pay the expenses to maintain it.

The multitude which crowds the stadium to watch a game, laugh and applaud, is a multitude of fools who are incapable of practicing sports themselves; they crowd the grandstands practicing lethargy and applaud those heroes who took the initiative, and who dominated the field and the sporting activities, and exploited all the offered means of supports sustained by the masses. The grandstands of public athletic fields are actually constructed to obstruct access to the fields. These grandstands shall one day be vacated and abolished when the masses march into athletic fields to practice sports in crowds, as they realize that sports are activities to be practiced not watched.

The grandstands shall disappear when no spectators come to fill up the rows and seats. People who are incapable of performing heroic acts in life, and those who are not well read in history and are incapable of visualizing the future, and those who do not take life seriously, are the marginal people who fill up the seats in theatres and other kinds of performances, to watch life events and learn how these events take their course. They are exactly like pupils who fill up the seats in schools because they are uneducated, because they are initially illiterate.

Those who make their own life do not need to see how life takes its course through watching the actors on stage or other theatres. Likewise, horsemen who ride their horses have no place on the sidelines of the racetrack, and if all people owned horses there would be no spectators to watch and applaud. The seated spectators are only those who cannot practice horse riding because they do not ride horses.

Thus Bedouin people are not interested in the theatre and other performances because they are hard working and take life very seriously. They are the makers of the serious life and that is why they look upon acting with scorn. Bedouin people also don't watch players playing a game; they practice their own games collectively and hold their own festivities, because they feel the spontaneous, inexplicable need for it.

The various kinds of boxing and wrestling are evidence that mankind has not yet purged the tendency to cruel behaviour. But this shall inevitably come to an end when man progresses and becomes more civilized. Gun matches and before that, human offerings were familiar practices in an earlier stage of human progress. But these cruel practices ended hundreds of years ago, and later, man came to look upon those practices with self-derision and distress too because human beings like himself had once indulged in such practices. It shall be the same with the various kinds of boxing and wrestling after decades or maybe hundreds of years. But the more civilized and the more progressive individuals are the only ones able to avoid such cruel practices and refrain from giving encouragement to those who indulge in them.